NO REGRETS

A 14-Day Devotional To Help You Move Forward

Shonareka Hunter

Table Of Contents

DAY 1:

Embracing Your Uniqueness 1

DAY 2:

Letting Go of Past Mistakes 9

DAY 3:

Cultivating Self-Compassion 14

DAY 4:

Building Healthy Relationships 19

DAY 5:

Finding Strength in Vulnerability 24

DAY 6:

Pursuing Your Passions 29

DAY 7:

Navigating Life's Transitions 34

DAY 8:

Gratitude and Contentment 39

DAY 9:

Discovering Inner Peace 44

DAY 10:

Overcoming Fear and Doubt 49

DAY 11:

Empowering Your Inner Voice 54

DAY 12:

Forgiveness and Healing 59

DAY 13:

Living on Purpose 64

DAY 14:

Embracing the Future with No Regrets 69

DAY 1:
Embracing Your Uniqueness

Scripture: Psalm 139:14 (NIV) –

I praise you because I am fearfully and wonderfully made; your works are wonderful, I know that full well."

Devotional: In the quiet moments of reflection, consider the depth of Psalm 139:14. "I praise you because I am fearfully and wonderfully made..." These words echo the divine craftsmanship of our Creator, a God who intentionally shaped each one of us with unparalleled precision and care. The psalmist acknowledges this profound truth, expressing gratitude for the intricate design that is uniquely theirs.

God's creativity knows no bounds. He didn't fashion us as mere replicas but as distinct individuals, each bearing a signature blend of quirks, talents, and imperfections. In this diversity lies the beauty of His creation. Every facet of who you are has a purpose—

a divine intention woven into the very fabric of your being.

Reflection Questions:

How does the recognition that you are fearfully and wonderfully made impact your perspective on self-worth?

_____
_____
_____
_____
_____
_____
_____
_____
_____
_____
_____
_____
_____
_____

Consider your quirks, talents, and imperfections. How do these aspects contribute to your uniqueness and the tapestry of God's design?

In what ways can celebrating your uniqueness bring a deeper sense of joy and purpose to your daily life?

Reflect on a time when you might have struggled to embrace your God-given uniqueness. How can you shift your perspective to see these aspects as intentional and purposeful?

As you go about your day, how can you actively choose to celebrate and express gratitude for the way God has fearfully and wonderfully made you?

_____

_____

_____

_____

May your reflection on Psalm 139:14 be a source of encouragement, reminding you that you are a masterpiece, intricately designed by the hands of a loving Creator. Embrace the unique masterpiece that is you, and let your life reflect the praise that acknowledges the wonder of God's craftsmanship.

Prayer: Heavenly Father, help me recognize and appreciate the beauty of my uniqueness. Show me how to use my gifts for your glory and the benefit of others.

Devotional Questions:

1. What makes you unique and special?

_____

_____

_____

_____

_____

_____

_____

2. How can you use your uniqueness to serve others?

3. What insecurities about your uniqueness do you need to release to God today?

DAY 2:

Letting Go of Past Mistakes

Scripture: 1 John 1:9 (NIV) –

If we confess our sins, he is faithful and just and will forgive us our sins and purify us from all unrighteousness."

Devotional:

In the journey of life, we often find ourselves burdened by the weight of our mistakes and the shadows of our past. The enemy whispers lies, convincing us that we are defined by our shortcomings and failures. However, God's Word offers a powerful truth that can set us free from the chains of guilt and shame.

1 John 1:9 reminds us of a profound promise: "If we confess our sins, he is faithful and just and will forgive us our sins and purify us from all unrighteousness." These words are a beacon of hope, a divine invitation to release the heavy load of our

mistakes and step into the freedom that comes from God's forgiveness.

God's faithfulness is unwavering. When we come before Him with a humble heart, acknowledging our faults and seeking His forgiveness, He responds with love and grace. There is no sin too great, no past too dark that God's mercy cannot reach. His forgiveness is not only an eraser of our transgressions but a purifier, cleansing us from all unrighteousness.

It's important to grasp the significance of this promise – that in God's eyes, our past does not define us. The slate is wiped clean, and we are given a fresh start. The grace extended to us is not a one-time offer but an ongoing gift that accompanies us on our journey of faith.

Today, let go of the shackles that bind you to your past. Embrace the forgiveness that God freely offers. Confess your sins with sincerity, knowing that His mercy is greater than any mistake you've made. As you release the burden of guilt, feel the weight lifting from your shoulders. God's love transforms our brokenness into a beautiful testimony of His grace.

Move forward with confidence, knowing that you are forgiven and purified. Your identity is not found in your mistakes but in the redemptive power of Christ's sacrifice. Embrace the freedom that comes from being a child of God, forgiven and loved beyond measure. As you journey through life, carry with you the assurance that God's mercy is a constant companion, guiding you towards a future filled with hope and purpose.

Prayer: Loving God, I lay my past mistakes at your feet. Thank you for your forgiveness and the chance to start anew.

Devotional Questions:

1. What past mistakes have been holding you back?

_____
_____
_____
_____
_____
_____
_____
_____
_____
_____
_____

2. How can you extend forgiveness to yourself as God does?

3. What steps can you take today to move beyond your past?

DAY 3:

Cultivating Self-Compassion

Scripture: Psalm 103:8 (NIV) –

The Lord is compassionate and gracious, slow to anger, abounding in love."

In the hustle and bustle of life, it's easy to forget the depth of God's compassion. Psalm 103:8 paints a beautiful picture of our heavenly Father – "The Lord is compassionate and gracious, slow to anger, abounding in love." These words are not just a description of God's character but an invitation for us to reflect that same compassion in our own lives.

It's common for us to be our harshest critics, dwelling on our mistakes and shortcomings. Yet, God's compassion extends far beyond our understanding. He is patient with us, slow to anger, and overflowing with love. In the same way, He calls us to mirror this compassion in our relationships, but also, crucially, in the way we treat ourselves.

Extend the same compassion to yourself that God so generously offers you. Recognize your worth, not based on your achievements or failures, but on the immeasurable love God has for you. As you navigate the challenges of life, remember that God's compassion is not contingent on your perfection but is freely given, embracing you in your brokenness.

In those moments when you stumble and fall short, be kind and patient with yourself. God's love is not reserved for the days when everything goes according to plan; it remains constant even in the midst of our shortcomings. Embrace the truth that you are a beloved child of God, deserving of the same compassion and grace He extends to you.

Take time to reflect on Psalm 103:8. Let the reality of God's compassion sink into the depths of your heart. As you meditate on His character, allow it to transform the way you view yourself. Replace self-condemnation with self-compassion, recognizing that you are a work in progress, and God's love is shaping and molding you into the person He created you to be.

Today, make a conscious effort to be kind to yourself. Embrace your journey with all its twists and turns, knowing that God's compassion is a guiding light, leading you to a place of healing, growth, and deeper intimacy with Him. As you extend compassion to yourself, you open the door to experience the fullness of God's love and grace in every aspect of your life.

Prayer: Heavenly Father, help me to see myself through your loving and compassionate eyes. Teach me to be gentle with myself.

Devotional Questions:

1. How can you show yourself more compassion and grace?

2. In what areas of your life do you tend to be harshest on yourself?

3. What is one practical way you can practice self-compassion today?

DAY 4:
Building Healthy Relationships

Scripture: Proverbs 17:17 (NIV) –

A friend loves at all times, and a brother is born for a time of adversity."

In the tapestry of life, relationships form the vibrant threads that weave through our journey. Proverbs 17:17 beautifully captures the essence of true friendship: "A friend loves at all times, and a brother is born for a time of adversity." This verse reminds us of the profound impact healthy relationships can have on our lives.

God designed us for connection, and meaningful relationships play a crucial role in our well-being. Friends who love unconditionally, who stand with us through the highs and lows, are treasures to be cherished. However, the verse goes beyond the ordinary and speaks of a brother born for adversity –

someone specifically designed to walk with us through challenges.

Reflect on your relationships. Are you surrounded by friends and companions who love you consistently? Do you have individuals in your life who are there not just for the good times but who stand by you in adversity? These are the connections that mirror God's intention for friendship.

Seek relationships that support, encourage, and love you in all seasons of life. Just as God places people in our lives for a purpose, we have a responsibility to choose wisely and cultivate connections that align with His design for healthy relationships. Pray for wisdom in discerning those who will be true friends and brothers, uplifting and guiding you on your journey.

Building and maintaining healthy relationships require intentionality. Take time in prayer to seek God's guidance. Ask Him to reveal the people He has placed in your life for a reason. Pray for discernment in recognizing the qualities of true friendship – love, loyalty, and support. And, in turn, ask for the strength and wisdom to be that kind of friend to others.

As you navigate the intricate tapestry of relationships, remember that you are not meant to walk this journey alone. God has gifted you with companions who love at all times and brothers or sisters born for times of adversity. Embrace these connections, nurture them, and give thanks for the richness they bring to your life.

May your relationships be a source of joy, strength, and mutual growth. May God's wisdom guide you in building bonds that reflect His love and grace. As you invest in healthy relationships, you'll discover the profound truth that we are not only created for God but also for one another, walking hand in hand through the various seasons of life.

Prayer: Lord, guide me in choosing and nurturing relationships that reflect your love and care.

Devotional Questions:

1. What qualities do you look for in a healthy relationship?

_____

_____

_____

_____

_____

_____

_____

2. Are there relationships in your life that need mending or strengthening?

3. How can you be a better friend or partner to those you care about?

DAY 5:
Finding Strength in Vulnerability

Scripture: 2 Corinthians 12:9 (NIV) –

But he said to me, 'My grace is sufficient for you, for my power is made perfect in weakness.'"

Devotional: In the tapestry of our lives, we often encounter moments of vulnerability—times when our own strength falters, and our weaknesses come to the forefront. It's during these seasons that the words of 2 Corinthians 12:9 offer a profound revelation: "My grace is sufficient for you, for my power is made perfect in weakness."

In a world that often values self-sufficiency and unyielding strength, the concept of finding perfection in weakness may seem counterintuitive. Yet, God's wisdom challenges us to view vulnerability not as a flaw but as a canvas on which His grace can paint a masterpiece of strength and resilience.

Consider the times in your life when you've felt most exposed, most fragile. These moments may be the very canvas upon which God desires to showcase His power. When we trust in God's strength during our moments of weakness, we open the door to transformative growth and deeper connections.

Vulnerability is not a sign of inadequacy but an acknowledgment of our need for something greater than ourselves. It's an invitation for God's grace to flood into the broken places, mending and strengthening us in ways we could never achieve on our own.

As you navigate the complexities of life, allow yourself to be vulnerable, trusting that God's grace is indeed sufficient. In those moments of weakness, when you feel the weight of your limitations, remember that His power is perfected in those very spaces. Your vulnerabilities become opportunities for God to showcase His strength.

Take a moment to reflect on the relationships in your life. Are there areas where you've hesitated to be vulnerable? Invite God into those spaces, asking for the courage to trust in His strength. Pray for the discernment to share your weaknesses with those you trust, fostering an environment of authenticity and support.

In embracing vulnerability, we position ourselves to experience the fullness of God's grace. His power is not hindered by our weaknesses; rather, it is magnified in them. Through the cracks of our vulnerabilities, the light of His strength shines brightly, illuminating a path of growth, resilience, and deeper connections.

May you find solace in the truth that God's grace is more than enough for you. In your moments of weakness, remember that His power is at its most potent, perfecting strength within you. Embrace vulnerability as a gateway to a richer, more authentic life, trusting in the promise that, through Christ, your weaknesses become a canvas for His perfect strength.

Prayer: Heavenly Father, grant me the courage to be vulnerable and find strength in my weaknesses.

Devotional Questions:

1. In what areas of your life is it challenging to be vulnerable?

_____

_____

_____

_____

_____

2. How has vulnerability led to growth or deeper relationships in the past?

3. How can you embrace vulnerability in your daily life?

DAY 6:

Pursuing Your Passions

Scripture: Colossians 3:23 (NIV) –

Whatever you do, work at it with all your heart, as working for the Lord, not for human masters."

In the rhythm of life, we are often presented with opportunities to engage our passions and invest our time and energy in pursuits that resonate with the desires of our hearts. Colossians 3:23 reminds us, "Whatever you do, work at it with all your heart, as working for the Lord, not for human masters."

Your passions are a gift from God, crafted uniquely within the fabric of your being. They are the sparks that ignite your spirit and fill your days with purpose. God's call is not for us to pursue our passions half-heartedly, but rather to dive into them wholeheartedly, recognizing that our endeavors are ultimately unto the Lord.

Reflect on the things that set your heart on fire, the activities that bring you joy and fulfillment. These passions are not arbitrary; they are woven into the very tapestry of who you are. The Creator has gifted you with unique talents, interests, and desires that, when pursued with dedication, become a form of worship.

As you engage in your daily work and pursue your passions, consider the motivation behind your efforts. Are you working merely for human approval, or are you directing your wholehearted commitment as an offering to the Lord? When we align our passions with God's purpose, even the most mundane tasks become opportunities for worship.

Take a moment to seek God's guidance in aligning your passions with His purpose. Pray for clarity and discernment as you navigate the path that sets your heart ablaze. Ask for wisdom to recognize the divine calling within your pursuits and the strength to persevere when challenges arise.

Remember that your wholehearted pursuit of your passions is an act of worship. Whether in your career, creative endeavors, or daily responsibilities, approach each task with the intention of glorifying God. When your heart is aligned with His purpose, you'll find fulfillment and joy beyond measure, for you are working not just for human approval but as an offering to the One who created you.

May your days be filled with the enthusiasm of pursuing what sets your heart on fire. In your wholehearted efforts, may you find God's purpose unfolding, bringing depth and meaning to every aspect of your life. As you work with all your heart, may it be a sweet offering to the Lord, a fragrant aroma of worship that rises from the canvas of your passions.

Prayer: Lord, reveal to me the passions you've placed in my heart and guide me in using them for your glory.

Devotional Questions:

1. What are your passions, and how can you pursue them more intentionally?

_____

_____

_____

_____

_____

_____

_____

_____

2. How might your passions be used to serve others and honor God?

3. What's one step you can take today to invest more in your passions?

DAY 7:

Navigating Life's Transitions

Scripture: Isaiah 43:18-19 (NIV) –

"Forget the former things; do not dwell on the past. See, I am doing a new thing! Now it springs up; do you not perceive it?"

Life is a journey marked by transitions, moments when the familiar shifts, and we find ourselves standing at the threshold of change. In these times, Isaiah 43:18-19 offers a powerful reminder: "Forget the former things; do not dwell on the past. See, I am doing a new thing! Now it springs up; do you not perceive it?"

As you navigate the ebb and flow of life's transitions, it's natural to carry the weight of past experiences. Yet, God invites us to release the grip of the familiar and embrace the new beginnings He is orchestrating. Transitions are opportunities for growth and fresh possibilities, and trusting God to lead you through each one is key to unlocking their potential.

Consider the times in your life when change has been accompanied by unexpected blessings or personal growth. Reflect on the ways God has led you through transitions in the past, providing strength, guidance, and clarity. His faithfulness in those moments serves as a foundation for your trust in His leading today.

Transitions can be challenging, often stirring a mix of emotions—excitement, uncertainty, and sometimes even fear. Yet, God's promise in Isaiah reminds us that He is actively at work, bringing forth a new thing. In the midst of change, He is sculpting opportunities for growth and new beginnings.

Trust is the cornerstone of navigating life's transitions with grace. Trust that God's plans for you are filled with hope and purpose, even when the path ahead seems unclear. Seek His wisdom in prayer, surrendering your fears and uncertainties into His capable hands. Allow Him to guide your steps, confident that His leading is always toward abundant life.

Open your heart to perceive the new things God is bringing into your life. Change, when surrendered to God's hands, becomes a journey of discovery and transformation. Instead of dwelling on what was, look forward with anticipation to what God is unfolding in the present and what He has prepared for your future.

As you trust God in life's transitions, may you find comfort in Isaiah 43:18-19. Embrace the new opportunities and growth that change can bring, allowing God to lead the way. His promise holds true: He is doing a new thing. May you perceive it with eyes of faith, stepping into the future with confidence, knowing that the One who makes all things new is guiding you with love and purpose..

Prayer: Gracious God, help me embrace the changes and transitions in my life, knowing that you are in control.

Devotional Questions:

1. What transitions are you currently facing in your life?

_____

_____

_____

_____

_____

_____

_____

_____

_____

2. How can you perceive God's guidance and new opportunities in these changes?

3. What can you do to find peace and stability in uncertain times?

DAY 8:

Gratitude and Contentment

Scripture: 1 Thessalonians 5:18 (NIV) –

Give thanks in all circumstances; for this is God's will for you in Christ Jesus."

In the tapestry of life, gratitude is the thread that weaves joy, contentment, and connection. 1 Thessalonians 5:18 encourages us with a powerful directive: "Give thanks in all circumstances; for this is God's will for you in Christ Jesus."

Cultivating a heart of gratitude is not contingent on our circumstances but is a choice we make, rooted in the recognition of God's goodness. In every situation, the invitation is extended to find something to be thankful for, for it is in gratitude that we align our hearts with God's will for our lives.

Consider the rhythm of your daily life. Are there moments of frustration, disappointment, or challenge that overshadow the blessings surrounding you? In the midst of life's ups and downs, the call to give thanks stands firm. Gratitude is not a denial of difficulties but a deliberate choice to focus on the goodness of God even in the face of adversity.

Contentment is born out of a heart that acknowledges and appreciates God's blessings, big and small. Take time each day to reflect on the gifts that grace your life—the relationships, the moments of joy, the lessons learned in trials. When we intentionally seek out reasons to be thankful, we open our hearts to the transformative power of gratitude.

In the face of hardships, the act of giving thanks may seem challenging, but it is precisely in those moments that gratitude becomes a lifeline. As you navigate difficulties, look for the glimmers of God's grace, the silver linings that remind you of His constant presence and care.

Pray for a heart that overflows with gratitude. Ask God to help you see His blessings in every circumstance, to shift your focus from what may be lacking to the abundance of His provision. Gratitude is a choice that leads to a deeper understanding of God's love and faithfulness.

Today, embrace the challenge and the joy of giving thanks in all circumstances. Let gratitude be the melody that accompanies your journey, weaving a harmonious connection between your heart and

God's will. As you recognize and appreciate the blessings in your life, may you find contentment, joy, and a profound sense of God's presence in every moment.

Prayer: Heavenly Father, fill my heart with gratitude and help me find contentment in your provision.

Devotional Questions:

1. How can you practice gratitude daily, even in challenging times?

2. What blessings are you thankful for today?

3. How does gratitude contribute to a sense of contentment in your life?

DAY 9:

Discovering Inner Peace

Scripture: Philippians 4:7 (NIV) –

And the peace of God, which transcends all understanding, will guard your hearts and your minds in Christ Jesus."

Devotional: In the midst of life's chaos and uncertainties, the pursuit of peace can feel like an elusive journey. Yet, Philippians 4:7 unveils a profound promise: "And the peace of God, which transcends all understanding, will guard your hearts and your minds in Christ Jesus."

True peace, the kind that surpasses comprehension, doesn't originate from the circumstances around us but flows from the very heart of God. It is a peace that goes beyond human reasoning, a tranquil assurance that we can find when we seek His presence amid life's tumultuous moments.

Consider the challenges and uncertainties you face today. Where do you turn in your search for peace?

Philippians 4:7 invites us to turn our gaze toward God. It is in His presence that we discover a peace that surpasses our understanding—a peace that stands firm in the face of chaos, offering comfort and assurance.

The pursuit of God's peace involves intentional moments of seeking His presence. In prayer, surrender your anxieties and concerns, laying them at the feet of the One who holds the universe in His hands. As you spend time in His Word, allow the truth of His promises to permeate your heart and mind, becoming an anchor in the storm.

The peace of God isn't contingent on the absence of challenges but is found in His nearness. Even when circumstances seem overwhelming, His peace acts as a guardian, protecting your heart and mind from the onslaught of fear and anxiety. It's a peace that assures you that, no matter what unfolds, you are held securely in the embrace of your Heavenly Father.

Today, intentionally seek the presence of God. Invite Him into the chaos of your day, allowing His peace to flow into the depths of your being. As you surrender your concerns to Him, may you experience the profound truth that His peace transcends all understanding. In the midst of life's uncertainties, may you find solace, assurance, and a steadfast calm that can only come from the God whose peace surpasses all understanding.

Prayer: Lord, grant me your peace that surpasses all understanding and guards my heart and mind.

Devotional Questions:

1. What typically disrupts your inner peace?

2. How can you invite God's peace into your daily life more consistently?

_____
_____
_____
_____
_____
_____
_____
_____
_____
_____
_____
_____
_____

3. What practices or habits can help you maintain inner peace?

_____
_____
_____

DAY 10:
Overcoming Fear and Doubt

Scripture: 2 Timothy 1:7 (NIV) –

"For the Spirit God gave us does not make us timid, but gives us power, love, and self-discipline."

Devotional: In the tapestry of life, fear and doubt often weave themselves into the fabric of our journey. Yet, 2 Timothy 1:7 reminds us of a powerful truth: "For the Spirit God gave us does not make us timid, but gives us power, love, and self-discipline."

Fear can manifest in various forms—fear of the unknown, fear of failure, or fear of inadequacy. Doubt can whisper lies, questioning our worth and abilities. However, as followers of Christ, we are not left to navigate these challenges on our own. God's Spirit within us is a source of courage, empowerment, and self-discipline.

Take a moment to reflect on the fears and doubts that may be present in your life. Are there situations or decisions that evoke timidity or uncertainty? 2

Timothy 1:7 is a beacon of assurance, reminding you that God has equipped you with a Spirit that imparts power, love, and self-discipline.

Trust in God's strength to face your fears with courage. The power of the Holy Spirit within you is not passive but dynamic, providing you with the strength to overcome every obstacle. Allow His power to embolden you, giving you the resilience to step into the unknown and face challenges with confidence.

God's love is a transformative force that casts out fear (1 John 4:18). As you navigate moments of doubt, anchor yourself in the love of God. His love is a constant, unchanging truth that dispels the lies of inadequacy. Rest in the assurance that you are deeply loved, and His perfect love casts out all fear.

Self-discipline, another gift from the Spirit, empowers you to take intentional steps in overcoming fear and doubt. Through prayer, reflection, and seeking God's guidance, cultivate the discipline to align your thoughts with His truth. The Spirit provides the strength to replace doubt with confidence and timidity with boldness.

Today, embrace the truth of 2 Timothy 1:7. Allow the Spirit of God within you to propel you forward with power, love, and self-discipline. As you face fears and doubts, trust in His strength, knowing that you are not alone in the journey. God's Spirit is your guide and companion, leading you with courage and assurance..

Prayer: Heavenly Father, help me overcome my fears and doubts with the power, love, and self-discipline you provide.

Devotional Questions:

1. What are your common sources of fear and doubt?

_____

_____

_____

_____

_____

_____

_____

_____

_____

_____

_____

2. How can you rely on God's strength to face these challenges?

3. What steps can you take to conquer your fears and doubts today?

DAY 11:
Empowering Your Inner Voice

Scripture: Proverbs 18:21 (NIV) –

The tongue has the power of life and death, and those who love it will eat its fruit."

Devotional: In the quiet recesses of your mind, your inner voice speaks a narrative that shapes your thoughts, feelings, and actions. Proverbs 18:21 underscores the profound truth that "the tongue has the power of life and death, and those who love it will eat its fruit."

Consider the words you speak to yourself internally—the silent dialogue that accompanies your daily life. The thoughts you entertain and the words you choose in your mind wield a significant influence over your perspective and behaviors. The power of life and death lies not only in the words you utter aloud but also in the conversations you hold within.

In the quiet moments of reflection, ask yourself: Does my inner voice speak life or death? Are my thoughts aligned with God's truth and love, or do they harbor negativity and self-doubt? Proverbs 18:21 challenges us to recognize the weight of our inner dialogue and choose words that bear the fruit of life.

Your inner voice is a powerful force that can either build you up or tear you down. Choose words of life and positivity, aligning your inner voice with the truth found in God's Word. Replace self-criticism with self-compassion, doubts with affirmations, and negativity with gratitude. Allow God's love to permeate your thoughts, cultivating a mindset that reflects His grace.

In the moments when doubt or negativity creeps in, intentionally redirect your inner dialogue. Speak God's promises over your life, reminding yourself of His love, grace, and purpose for you. When faced with challenges, let your inner voice be a source of encouragement and strength, echoing the truth that you are more than a conqueror in Christ (Romans 8:37).

Today, commit to cultivating a positive and life-giving inner voice. As you align your thoughts with God's truth, you will find that the fruit it bears is rich with joy, peace, and confidence. Choose words that speak life, not only over others but also over yourself. In doing so, you participate in the transformative work of God's Word, allowing His love to shape every aspect of your being.

Prayer: Lord, help me use my words to speak life and encouragement to myself and others.

Devotional Questions:

1. How does your inner voice typically speak to you?

_____
_____
_____
_____
_____
_____
_____
_____
_____
_____
_____
_____
_____

2. In what ways can you align your inner voice with God's truth and love?

_____

_____

_____

_____

_____

_____

_____

_____

_____

_____

_____

_____

_____

3. How can you use your words to lift others up today?

_____

_____

_____

DAY 12:

Forgiveness and Healing

Scripture: Colossians 3:13 (NIV) –

Bear with each other and forgive one another if any of you has a grievance against someone. Forgive as the Lord forgave you."

Devotional: In the complex tapestry of relationships, Colossians 3:13 serves as a guiding light: "Bear with each other and forgive one another if any of you has a grievance against someone. Forgive as the Lord forgave you." These words unveil a powerful truth—forgiveness is not just a choice; it is a transformative act that brings healing both to you and to others.

The command to forgive is not an invitation to minimize the pain or dismiss the wrongdoing. Rather, it is an acknowledgment that harboring grievances can weigh heavy on the soul, hindering our growth and impeding the harmony God desires for our relationships.

Consider any grievances you may be carrying—the hurts, the disappointments, the lingering pain. Colossians 3:13 invites you to release the burden of unforgiveness. In doing so, you follow the example set by the Lord, who forgave you in the midst of your own shortcomings and failures.

Forgiveness is not an endorsement of the wrong done; rather, it is a deliberate choice to free yourself and the other person from the chains of bitterness. As you extend forgiveness, you open the door to healing, allowing God's grace to mend the broken places and restore relationships.

Reflect on the ways the Lord has forgiven you. His forgiveness is not dependent on our merit but flows from His boundless love and grace. In the same way, let your forgiveness be an extension of God's love, reflecting His mercy and compassion.

Release the grip of unforgiveness today. Take a step toward healing by forgiving those who have hurt you. Surrender your grievances to God, trusting that His grace is more than sufficient to mend the wounds and restore peace. As you forgive, you not only follow the example set by the Lord but also open the door to a renewed sense of freedom, joy, and reconciliation.

In the act of forgiveness, you participate in God's transformative work, allowing His love to permeate your relationships. May you experience the profound healing that forgiveness brings, both to your heart and to the lives you touch. As you forgive as the Lord forgave you, may His grace flow abundantly, bringing restoration and a deeper understanding of the power of His love.

Prayer: Loving God, grant me the grace to forgive as you've forgiven me, and bring healing to my heart.

Devotional Questions:

1. Are there unresolved grudges or unforgiveness in your life?

_____
_____
_____
_____
_____
_____
_____
_____
_____
_____

2. How can you practice forgiveness, even in difficult circumstances?

3. What steps can you take today to begin the process of forgiveness and healing?

DAY 13:
Living on Purpose

Scripture: Ephesians 2:10 (NIV) –

For we are God's handiwork, created in Christ Jesus to do good works, which God prepared in advance for us to do."

Devotional: In the intricacies of creation, God has crafted each of us with purpose and intention. Ephesians 2:10 unfolds a profound truth: "For we are God's handiwork, created in Christ Jesus to do good works, which God prepared in advance for us to do." This verse invites us to embark on a journey of discovering and fulfilling our unique calling.

Reflect on the idea that you are God's handiwork, a masterpiece created with care and precision. Just as an artist meticulously shapes a sculpture, God has crafted you for a purpose. Your life is not a random occurrence; it is a deliberate design fashioned by the Creator's hands.

Consider the good works that God has prepared in advance for you to do. Your purpose is not an afterthought but a part of God's intentional plan. Seek His guidance to discover the unique calling He has placed on your life. Pray for wisdom and discernment to recognize the path He has prepared for you.

Living with purpose involves aligning your life with God's plan. It requires seeking His guidance daily, surrendering your plans and desires to His will. When you live each day with intention, you step into the good works God has prepared for you, making a positive impact on the world around you.

Take a moment to reflect on your daily actions. Are you living with a sense of purpose, aware that each day presents an opportunity to fulfill God's plan? Seek His guidance in prayer, asking for clarity and courage to walk in the path He has laid out for you.

Embrace the assurance that you are a significant part of God's grand design. Your life, your talents, and your experiences are woven into the tapestry of His purpose. As you seek to fulfill the good works He has prepared for you, you contribute to the unfolding story of His redemptive love.

Today, live with the knowledge that you are God's handiwork, created for a purpose. Seek His guidance to discover and fulfill the unique calling on your life. Approach each day with intention, knowing that you are contributing to God's plan and making a difference in the world. May your life be a reflection of His glory as you live out the purpose for which you were created.

Prayer: Lord, reveal your purpose for my life and guide me in fulfilling it with passion and dedication.

Devotional Questions:

1. What passions or talents align with your sense of purpose?

_____
_____
_____
_____
_____
_____
_____
_____
_____
_____
_____

2. In what ways can you actively pursue your purpose daily?

3. How can you make a positive impact on the world around you?

DAY 14:

Embracing the Future with No Regrets

Scripture: Jeremiah 29:11 (NIV) –

For I know the plans I have for you, declares the Lord, plans for welfare and not for evil, to give you a future and a hope."

Devotional: In the journey of life, uncertainties can often cast shadows over our path. In those moments, Jeremiah 29:11 stands as a beacon of hope: "For I know the plans I have for you, declares the Lord, plans for welfare and not for evil, to give you a future and a hope." This verse invites us to trust in God's unfolding plan for our lives.

Reflect on the assurance that God knows the plans He has for you. Your life is not a series of random events; it is a narrative written by the Creator Himself. As you navigate the twists and turns of your journey, hold onto the promise that His plans are for your welfare, offering a future filled with hope.

Embrace your uniqueness, recognizing that God has crafted you with purpose. Your talents, experiences, and passions are intricately woven into the tapestry of His design. Trust that the One who knows the plans for your life has equipped you with everything you need to fulfill them.

Let go of the weight of the past. Whether it's mistakes, missed opportunities, or regrets, release them into God's hands. His plans for you are not hindered by your past but are designed to lead you toward a hopeful future. Seek His forgiveness, accept His grace, and move forward with confidence.

Pursue your passions with a sense of purpose. God's plans for you include the things that set your heart on fire. As you align your pursuits with His will, you step into the fullness of the future and hope He has prepared for you. Pray for guidance and wisdom, trusting that He will direct your steps.

Today, move forward with no regrets. Embrace the hope that comes from trusting in God's plans for your life. As you journey with Him, you can be confident that your future is secure in His hands. Walk in the knowledge that the Creator of the universe has mapped out a hopeful and purposeful path for you.

In the moments of uncertainty, hold onto Jeremiah 29:11. Trust in the plans God has for you, plans that lead to welfare and hope. As you walk in step with Him, may your heart be filled with assurance, peace, and anticipation for the bright future He has lovingly prepared for you.

Prayer: Gracious Father, I entrust my future to your care and guidance, knowing you have plans for my welfare and a hopeful future.

Devotional Questions:

1. What steps can you take to face the future with confidence and trust in God's plan?

_____
_____
_____
_____
_____
_____
_____
_____
_____
_____
_____

2. What dreams or goals do you want to pursue without regrets?

3. How can you continue to apply the lessons learned in this devotional to your future journey?

___

May you embrace each day with purpose, live without regrets, and find peace and fulfillment in your walk with God.

Made in the USA
Columbia, SC
14 April 2025